How to Smoke Meat

Over 25 Delicious Smoked Meat Recipes for Your Next Family Barbecue

By

Ted Alling

License Notes

Table of Contents

Introduction

Smoking your own meat is very different from barbecuing. When you smoke meat you often have to look at it as slow cooking your meal as if you were cooking it in a slow cooker. Of course there are many of us who will have their own preferences and our own special equipment that we will use for smoking, but for the average novice out there, they will not know where to even begin.

That is something I hope to change inside of this book. This book is meant to be an informal guide for not just the novice smoker, but also can be used by those experienced in smoking meat. Inside of this book you will discover a thorough and in-depth guide to smoking your own meat from the comfort of your own home as well as over 25 of the most delicious smoked meat recipes that will help accomplish just that and more.

So, let's not waste any more time.

Let's get smoking!

Top Ten Tips for Smoking Your Meat

One of the most favorite past times for many people during the summer time months other than sports has become smoking their own meat. There is just nothing quite like the aroma of wood smoked meat wafting from your backyard that is just as pleasing. While each home chef out there may have their own methods that they use for smoking their meat, it is not a difficult skill to master. In this section I want to give you a few helpful tips to ensure that you are making some of the most delicious smoked meat meals you and your family will ever taste.

Tip 1: Always Start Early

When it comes to smoking meat, one of the best things that you can do to ensure that your meat has a whopping amount of flavor is to start prepping carly. If you want your meat to start absorbing all of the smoky flavors as soon as possible, it is best to start prepping your meat while it is still raw. This is when you will want to rush your meat into your smoker as soon as possible. Keep in mind the longer that your meat is sitting out, the more dried out it will become.

Tip 2: Always Cook Your Meat Slowly

When you taste real barbecue for yourself, you will soon be able to see that it is not made by smothering barbecue sauce all over your meat. The real secret to authentic barbecue is slow cooking your meat over low heat for a certain number of hours. This is the way that most authentic barbecued meat is always moist and tender and this is something that you will want to keep in mind when you are smoking your own meat.

Tip 3: Regulate the Heat Inside of Your Smoker with a Pan Filled with Water

When you have enormous fluctuations in temperature in the inside of your smoker, it can cause your meat to become too tight or to dry out. The best way to avoid this from happening is to use a pan filled with water and set it into the inside of your smoker. This pan of water will help to stabilize the heat inside of your smoker and even add some humidity that will help keep your meat moist and tender.

Tip 4: Never Overdo It

One of the biggest mistakes that many novice smokers tend to make is overdoing it. They tend to add way too many woodchips to their smoker or overdo it on the seasoning. The rule of thumb to follow when it comes to smoking is to only smoke your meat no longer than half of its required cooking time. Do this and your meat will come out tasting delicious each and every time.

Tip 5: Remember, Black Smoke Is a Bad Thing

When you are smoking your meat, you may notice a few puffs of white smoke escaping your smoker. White smoke is a good sign as it means that your meat is being layered with that intoxicating smoky flavor that you love. However, if you begin to notice black smoke coming out of your smoker, this is a bad sign. This can be caused for a variety of different reasons such as your smoker not getting the proper ventilation or that your food is being cooked directly over the fire. The rule of thumb to follow is always strive for your smoker to have white smoke. Avoid black smoke.

Tip 6: Always Keep the Air Flowing

The most important thing that you can do while your meat is smoking is to ensure proper ventilation during the cooking process. While your meat is smoking, you want to make sure that you keep the vents of your grill or smoker open at all times. This will help to draw smoke from your charcoal or woodchips and cause it to swirl around your food while coming out of the top properly.

Tip 7: Never Leave Your Smoker Unattended

While it is true that smoking meat requires many hours of your time, it does not mean that you should ever leave your smoker unattended during this time. You want to ensure a safe cooking environment so with that said always check on the temperature of your smoker every hour or two to make sure that your smoker isn't reaching dangerous levels.

Tip 8: Don't Peek At Your Food As It Is Cooking

One thing that you may have to fight yourself on is peaking at your food as it cooks. You need to keep in mind that every time you open your grill or smoker, it will cause it to lose heat and add even more time onto the cooking process. With that said never peek at your food just to see how it is coming along. Only open your grill or smoker if you need to add in more woodchips, tend to the fire inside, add a water pan or check the doneness of your meat as it nears the end of its cooking time.

Tip 9: Make Sure That Your "Bark" Darkens Just Right

The sign of truly authentic barbecued and smoked meat is for it to have that special glisten with a dark brown crust that we all love and wish for. This is known as the "bark" of your meat and is the signature of good smoking. Before you take off your meat out of your smoker once it has reach the end of it cooking time, you want to make sure that the "bark" on the surface is just the right shade of mahogany brown to ensure it tastes just like a little slice of heaven.

Tip 10: Always Spice Your Meat Just Right

The key main ingredients of any perfect smoked recipe is that every flavor should play a role in h overall taste. You want to make sure that you don't have one flavor that overshadows the rest and instead strive to have the perfect balance between all of your spices.

Savory Smoked Meat Recipes

Smoked Mojo Leg Quarters

To kick things off we have a savory and easy smoked meat recipe that I know you are going to want to make as often as possible. Serve this with some relish and a side of mashed potatoes for the tastiest results.

Makes: 6 Servings

Total Prep Time: 6 Hours

Ingredients:

- 1/3 Cup of Olive Oil, Extra Virgin Variety
- 1 Tbsp. of Orange Zest, Fresh and Packed
- 1 Tbsp. of Lime Zest, Fresh and Packed
- 1/3 Cup of Orange Juice, Fresh
- ¼ Cup of Lime Juice, Fresh
- 1 Bunch of Cilantro, Fresh and Chopped
- 6 Cloves of Garlic, Minced
- 2 Jalapeno Peppers, Red in Color and Seeded
- ¼ Cup of Oregano Leaves, Fresh
- 1 ¼ tsp. of Cumin, Ground Variety
- 1 tsp. of Salt, For Taste
- ½ tsp. of Black Pepper, For Taste
- 6 Chicken Legs, Cut Into Quarters
- 6 Cups of Smoker Chips, Applewood Variety

Directions:

1. the first thing that you will want to do is add your olive oil, fresh orange and lime zest, fresh orange juice, fresh cilantro, minced garlic, jalapeno peppers, fresh oregano leaves, ground cumin and dash of salt and black pepper into a food processor. Pulse on the highest setting until thoroughly chopped. Reserve at least half a cup of this mixture for later use.

2. Next place your chicken into a large sized bowl and add in your remaining chopped mixture. Toss thoroughly to coat on all sides.

3. Cover your chicken with a sheet of plastic wrap and place into your fridge to chill for the next 4 to 8 hours.

4. Then place at least 3 cups of your Applewood chips into a sheet of aluminum foil. Wrap to form an envelope and repeat until all of your chips have been covered. Poke several holes in each packet that you make.

5. Light one side of your grill to at least 350 to 400 degrees. Make sure that you leave the other side of your grill unlit. Place at least one packet of your chips on the lit side and cover.

6. Pat your chicken legs with a paper towel to dry off the excess moisture, making sure to leave the marinade on the skin of your chicken. Season your chicken with a dash of salt and black pepper. Move your chip packet to the unlit side of your grill.

7. Grill your chicken for the next 4 to 6 minutes. After this time transfer your chicken to the unlit side of your grill and place your chip packed back onto the lit side.

8. Cover your grill and allow to cook for the next hour and 30 minutes, making sure to turn your chicken pieces and chip packet often.

9. After this time remove your chicken from the grill and set aside to stand for at least 10 minutes before serving.

Cowboy Style Brisket Sandwich

This is the perfect sandwich recipe to make whenever you are looking to feed your inner cowboy. Top this sandwich dish with your favorite toppings to make it truly unique.

Makes: 4 Servings

Total Prep Time: 10 Minutes

Ingredients:

- 8 Slices of Bread, Thick Cut
- 4 Slices of Cheese, Pepper Jack Variety
- 2 Cups of Beef Brisket, Finely Chopped and Presmoked
- Some Slices of Jalapeno Pepper, Pickled Variety

Directions:

1. The first thing that you will want to do is preheat your oven to 400 degrees.

2. While your oven is heating up place your bread slices onto a large sized baking sheet. Top these bread slices with some Pepper Jack cheese.

3. Place into your oven to bake for the next 5 minutes or until your bread is lightly toasted and your cheese is fully melted.

4. Remove from your oven and top these slices off with your cooked beef brisket, jalapeno pepper splices and remaining bread slices.

5. Serve right away and enjoy.

Easy Smoked Pork Chops

If you are a huge fan of pork chops, then this is one smoked recipe I know you are going to fall in love with. Easy to put together and made with a buttermilk BBQ sauce marinade that is going to leave your mouth watering.

Makes: 4 Servings

Total Prep Time: 4 Hours and 25 Minutes

Ingredients:

- 4 Tbsp. of Salt, For Favorite Kind
- 2 Tbsp. of Black Pepper, For Taste
- 2 Tbsp. of Brown Sugar, Light and Packed

- 2 Tbsp. of Thyme, Ground Variety
- 2 Tbsp. of Onion, Powdered Variety
- 1 Tbsp. of Cayenne Pepper, For Taste
- 4 Pork Chops, Bone in Variety and Center Cut Variety
- Some Applewood Chips, Soaked For At Least an Hour

Ingredients for Your Buttermilk BBQ Sauce:

- 1 Cup of Cider, Apple Variety
- 1 Tbsp. of Brown Sugar, Light and Packed
- ½ Cup of BBQ Sauce, Your Favorite Kind
- 1 Tbsp. of Buttermilk, Whole

Directions:

1. First use a small sized bowl and add in your dash of salt, dash of black pepper, light brown sugar, fresh thyme, powdered onion and dash of cayenne pepper. Stir thoroughly to combine. Rub this mixture over your pork chops.

2. Wrap your pork chops in a sheet of plastic wrap and set into your fridge to marinate for the next couple of hours.

3. While your meat is marinating preheat your grill to 275 degrees. Add in your soaked Applewood chips and cover.

4. Once your grill is hot enough add your pork chops to your grill. Cover and allow to smoke for the next hour and 10 minutes or until your pork chops are firm to the touch. After this time transfer your pork to a plate and allow to stand for at least 5 minutes.

5. While your pork chops are cook making your barbecue sauce. To do this use a medium sized saucepan and place over low to medium heat. Add in your apple cider and light brown sugar. Stir thoroughly to combine.

6. Cook your brown sugar mixture for at least 25 minutes before reducing the heat to low. Add in your favorite kind of barbecue sauce and stir well until incorporated evenly. Cook for another 5 minutes before adding in your buttermilk. Continue to cook for the next 5 minutes or until piping hot. Remove from heat.

7. Serve your pork chops with your freshly made barbecue sauce and enjoy.

Delicious Smoked Swordfish Smothered in White Clam Garlic Sauce

If you are a huge fan seafood, then this is one seafood dish that will be a hit in your household. While it may take a bit of time to put together, the end result is well worth the wait and effort.

Makes: 6 Servings

Total Prep Time: 15 Hours and 35 Minutes

Ingredients for Your Smoked Swordfish:

- 1 Cup of Salt, For Taste
- 1 Cup of Sugar, White in Color
- 2 Tbsp. of Peppercorns, Black in Color
- 1 Loin of Swordfish, Skin Removed
- 2 to 3 Tbsp. of Oil, Canola Variety

Ingredients for Your White Clam Sauce:

- 24 Clams, Littleneck Variety
- 2 Tbsp. of Oil, Canola Variety
- 3 Cloves of Garlic, Mashed Into A Paste
- 1 Chile, Serrano Variety, Small in Size and Finely Diced
- 1 Cup of White Wine, Your Favorite Kind
- 1 Tbsp. of Butter, Cold and Unsalted Variety
- 2 Tbsp. of Parsley, Fresh and Roughly Chopped
- 1 Lemon, Fresh and Zest Only
- Dash of Salt and Black Pepper, For Taste

Directions:

1. First make your swordfish. To do this use a large sized pot and add in at least 8 cups of water, dash of salt, white sugar and black peppercorns. Stir to combine and set over medium heat. Bring this mixture to a boil and continue to boil until your sugar fully dissolves. Remove from heat and allow to cool completely.

2. Once your mixture is cool add in your swordfish and allow to marinate in your fridge to chill for the next 12 hours.

3. After this time remove your swordfish and rinse under some running water. Pat dry with a few paper towels and allow to dry for the next hour.

4. While your fish is drying prepare your smoker. To do this add in a handful of your Applewood chips and allow your smoker to reach 200 to 225 degrees.

5. Brush your swordfish loin with a generous amount of oil and season with a touch of salt and black pepper. Transfer to your smoker and allow to smoke for the next 2 hours.

6. During this time make your clam sauce. To do this remove the meat from your clams and chop finely. Then heat up some oil in a medium sized saucepan placed over high heat. Once your oil is hot enough add in your garlic and chile. Cook for at least one minute before adding in your finely chopped clams. Continue to cook for an additional minute.

7. Add in your wine and bring your mixture to a simmer. Cook until your mixture is reduced by at least half.

8. After this time add in your whole clams and cover. Cook for the next 5 to 10 minutes or until the clams open on their own accord. Toss out any clams that do not open.

9. Add in your butter and stir thoroughly to combine. Remove from heat and add in your roughly chopped parsley and fresh lemon zest.

10. Pour this sauce over your smoked swordfish. Garnish with your fresh parsley leaves and enjoy right away.

Smoked Ginger Chicken with Cinnamon and Cardamom

This is a great smoked recipe to serve up whenever you are looking to impress your friends and family during your next dinner event. Relatively easy for a smoked meal, it is packed full of a delicious taste that I know you won't be able to resist.

Makes: 4 Servings

Total Prep Time: 2 Hours and 55 Minutes

Ingredients:

- 1 Tbsp. of Cloves, Whole
- 10 Cardamom, Pods Only
- 5 Sticks of Cinnamon
- 2 Tbsp. of Oil, Canola Variety
- 1 Piece of Ginger, Chopped Coarsely
- 1 Head of Garlic, With Cloves Removed
- 1 tsp. of Mustard Seeds, Black In Color
- Dash of Salt and Black Pepper, For Taste
- 1 Lime, Fresh, Juice and Zest Only
- 1, 3 Pound Chicken, Cut Butterfly Style and Keel Bone Removed

Directions:

1. Use a medium sized bowl and add in your whole cloves, pods of cardamom and sticks of cinnamon. Stir to combine and cover with some cold water. Allow to soak for at least one hour.

2. Then use a medium sized skillet and add in your oil. Set over medium heat. Once your oil is hot enough add in your ginger and garlic. Cook for the next 2 minutes or until they are soft to the touch.

3. Add in your mustard seeds and continue to cook for another 30 seconds.

4. Add in at least half a cup of water, your fresh lime zest and lime juice. Season with a dash of salt and black pepper. Bring this mixture to a boil and continue to cook for another minute.

5. Transfer this mixture to a blender. Blend on the highest setting until smooth in color. Remove and allow to cool slightly.

6. Rub this freshly made paste over your chicken, making sure to get under the skin. Cover your chicken with a sheet of aluminum foil and place into your fridge to chill for the next hour. After this time remove and allow to sit at room temperature for at least 10 minutes.

7. Preheat a smoker with some Applewood chips until it reaches 300 to 350 degrees. Once your smoker is hot enough add in your chicken and cook with the skin side facing down. Cook for at least 40 to 50 minutes or until your chicken is fully cooked through.

8. Remove and allow to stand for at least 10 minutes before carving.

Hearty Smoked Ribs Smothered in a Carolina BBQ Sauce

This is the ultimate smoked recipe if you are a huge fan of barbecue ribs. Smothered in a savory Carolina style barbecue sauce, this is one dish that I know you are going to want to make as often as possible.

Makes: 4 Servings

Total Prep Time: 19 Hours and 15 Minutes

Ingredients for Your Rub:

- ¼ Cup of Chili Powder, Ancho Variety
- 2 Tbsp. of Paprika, Spanish Variety
- 2 Tbsp. of Black Pepper, For Taste
- 2 Tbsp. of Mustard, Dried Variety
- 2 Tbsp. of Salt, For Taste
- 2 Tbsp. of Coriander, Ground Variety
- 1 Tbsp. of Oregano, Dried Variety
- 1 Tbsp. of Cumin, Ground Variety
- 2 tsp. of Chile de Arbol
- 2 Racks of Pork Ribs, St. Louis Style and Membrane Removed
- ¼ Cup of Oil, Canola Variety

Ingredients for Your Mop:

- 2 Cups of Vinegar, Cider Variety
- 2 Tbsp. of Brown Sugar, Light and Packed
- ½ tsp. of Cayenne, Powdered Variety
- Dash of Hot Sauce, Your Favorite Kind

- 1 Tbsp. of Salt, For Taste
- ¼ tsp. of Black Pepper, For Taste
- Some Wood Chips, Hickory and Applewood Variety
- 1 Quart of Cider, Apple Variety

Ingredients for Your Carolina BBQ Sauce:

- ¼ Cup of Oil, Canola Variety
- 2 Onions, Spanish Variety and Chopped Coarsely
- 6 Cloves of Garlic, Chopped Coarsely
- 2 Cups of Ketchup
- 2/3 Cup of Water, Warm
- ¼ Cup of Chili, Ancho Variety and Powdered Variety
- 2 Tbsp. of Paprika
- 2/3 Cup of Mustard, Dijon Variety
- 2/3 Cup of Vinegar, Cider Variety
- 2 Tbsp. of Worcestershire Sauce

- 2 Chipotle Chiles in Adobo, Canned Variety and Chopped Finely
- ¼ Cup of Brown Sugar, Dark in Color
- 2 Tbsp. of Honey, Raw
- 2 Tbsp. of Molasses
- Dash of Salt and Black Pepper, For Taste

Directions:

1. The first thing that you will want to do is use a medium sized bowl and add in all of your ingredients for your rub into it. Stir thoroughly to combine. Cover with a sheet of plastic wrap and place into your fridge to marinate for the next 12 hours.

2. Then use a large sized pot placed over low heat. Add in all of your ingredients for your mop and stir thoroughly to combine. Bring this mixture to a simmer and cook for at least 5 minutes or until the sugar is fully dissolved. Remove from heat and allow to cool completely.

3. Remove your ribs from your fridge and add in your chips to a smoker. Preheat your smoker to 220 degrees. Then place your cider into a small sized grill proof pan and place into your smoker.

4. Place your ribs into your smoker and cover. Smoke for the next 6 hours, making sure to brush your ribs with your mop mixture every hour. During the last hour of smoking brush your rubs with your barbecue sauce every 10 minutes.

5. To make your barbecue sauce heat some oil over medium to high heat in a large sized skillet. Once your oil is hot enough add in your onions and cook for the next 3 minutes or until the onions are soft to the touch. Once soft add in your garlic and continue to cook for an additional minute.

6. Add in your ketchup and water and stir to combine. Bring this mixture to a boil before reducing the heat to low. Allow to simmer for another 5 minutes.

7. Add in your remaining ingredients and stir thoroughly to evenly mix. Cook for at least 10 minutes or until your mixture is thick in consistency.

8. Transfer to a food processor and blend on the highest setting until smooth in consistency. Season this sauce with a touch of salt and black pepper.

9. Remove your ribs from your smoker and serve alongside with your barbecue sauce. Serve whenever you are ready and enjoy.

Classic Smoked Salmon

If you are a huge fan of traditional salmon, then this is the perfect smoked recipe for you to make. It is packed full of an authentic smoky flavor that you will want to enjoy over and over again.

Makes: 20 to 30 Servings

Total Prep Time: 29 Hours and 30 Minutes

Ingredients:

- 1 Cup of Salt, For Taste
- ½ Cup of Sugar, White in Color
- ½ Cup of Brown Sugar, Dark in Color and Packed
- 1 Tbsp. of Peppercorns, Black in Color and Crushed
- 2 Salmon Fillets, Large in Size and Pin Bones Removed

Directions:

1. Use a medium sized bowl and add in your dash of salt, white sugar, dark brown sugar and black peppercorns. Stir to combine.

2. Place a sheet of plastic wrap over a sheet of aluminum foil. Sprinkle your herb mixture over your plastic wrap. Lay your fish on your mixture with the skin side facing down. Sprinkle at least 1/3 of your rub mixture onto the other side of your salmon. Repeat with your remaining salmon fillet.

3. Fold your plastic wrap and aluminum foil sheet over your salmon. Crimp the edges to seal.

4. Allow your fish to marinate while being weighed down with a heavy plank for at least 12 hours. After this time remove the plank and flip your fish over.

5. After this time unwrap your fish and rinse off under some running water. Pat dry with a few paper towels and allow to dry for at least 1 to 3 hours.

6. Place some hardwood chips into a smoker and allow your smoker to reach 150 to 220 degrees. Place your salmon into your smoker and cover. Allow to cook until your fish reaches 150 degrees in internal temperature.

7. Remove after this time and serve whenever you are ready.

Oklahoma Style Flat Smoked Brisket

This is a traditional smoked brisket recipe that you can find being served in many authentic barbecue roadhouses. With the help of this recipe you can make this delicious brisket from the comfort of your own home.

Makes: 4 to 6 Servings

Total Prep Time: 7 Hours and 30 Minutes

Ingredients:

- ¼ Cup of Salt, For Taste
- ¼ Cup of Sugar, White in Color
- 2 Tbsp. of Garlic, Powdered Variety
- 2 Tbsp. of Onion, Powdered Variety
- 2 Tbsp. Paprika, Spanish Variety
- 2 Tbsp. of Chili, Powdered Variety
- 1 Tbsp. of Salt, Celery Variety
- 1 Tbsp. of Pepper, Lemon Variety
- 1 Tbsp. of Black Pepper, For Taste
- 1 Tbsp. of White Pepper, For Taste
- 1 tsp. of Cayenne Pepper
- 1, 5 to 8 Pound Beef Brisket, Flat Cut Variety
- 4 Cups of Wood Chips, Oak or Hickory Variety and Soaked
- 1 Cup of Apple Juice, Fresh
- 1 ½ Cups of BBQ Sauce, Your Favorite Kind

Directions:

1. Use a small sized bowl and add in your dash of salt, powdered garlic, powdered onion, Spanish style paprika, powdered chili, celery style salt, lemon pepper, dash of black pepper, dash of white pepper and cayenne pepper. Stir thoroughly together.

2. Rub your spice mixture all over your meat and cover the meat with a sheet of plastic wrap. Place into your fridge to sit for the next hour.

3. While your meat is sitting in your fridge preheat your smoker to 200 to 225 degrees. Place your woodchips into your smoke and cover.

4. Once your smoker is preheated add your meat to your smoker and cook for the 4 to 5 hours, making sure to add more woodchips every 2 hours. After this time remove your brisket and cover with some aluminum foil.

5. Place your brisket back onto your smoker and continue to smoke for an additional hour or two. Remove and allow to rest for the next 45 minutes. Slice and serve your favorite kind of barbecue sauce.

Texas Style Spicy Smoked Brisket

Just as the name implies this is one smoked recipe that you will be able to find throughout many authentic BBQ restaurants around Texas. Spiced with the perfect amount of spices, this is a brisket dish with a touch of spice that I know you are going to love.

Makes: 8 Servings

Total Prep Time: 15 Hours and 50 Minutes

Ingredients:

- 3 Tbsp. of Chile, Ancho Variety and Powdered Variety
- 2 Tbsp. of Salt, For Taste
- 1 Tbsp. of Allspice, Ground Variety
- 1 Tbsp. of Celery Seeds, Fresh
- 1 Tbsp. of Coriander Seeds, Ground Variety
- 1 Tbsp. of Garlic, Powdered Variety
- 1 Tbsp. of Mustard Seeds, Ground Variety
- 1 Tbsp. of Oregano, Dried
- 1 Tbsp. of Paprika, Spanish Variety and Smoked
- 1 Tbsp. of Black Pepper, For Taste
- 1, 8 to 10 Pound Brisket, Untrimmed Variety
- 3 Cups of Woodchips, Oak or Pecan Variety
- 2 Cups of Apple Juice, Fresh
- Some Barbecue Sauce, Your Favorite Kind

Ingredients for Your Texas Toast:

- 2 tsp. of Oil, Canola Variety
- 4 Cloves of Garlic, Smashed and Finely Chopped
- 2 Sticks of Butter, Unsalted Variety and Soft
- Dash of Salt and Black Pepper, For Taste
- 2 Loaves of Bread, Pullman Variety and Sliced Into Thick Slices
- 2 Tbsp. of Parsley, Flat Leaf Variety and Roughly Chopped

Ingredients for Your Pickled Red Onions:

- 1 ½ Cups of Vinegar, Red Wine Variety
- 2 Tbsp. of Sugar, White in Color
- 1 tsp. of Mustard Seeds, Fresh
- Dash of Salt, For Taste
- 1 Red Onion, Small in Size, Cut Into Halves and Sliced Thinly

Directions:

1. Use a small sized bowl and add in your powdered ancho chile, dash of salt, ground allspice, celery seeds, ground coriander seeds, powdered garlic, ground mustard seeds, dried oregano, smoked paprika and dash of black pepper. Stir thoroughly to combine.

2. Rub this mixture all over your brisket on all sides and wrap your brisket in a sheet of plastic wrap. Place into your fridge to chill for the next 4 hours. After this time remove your brisket from the fridge.

3. Preheat your smoker to 225 degrees with some soaked woodchips.

4. Once your smoker is preheated add your brisket and close your smoker. Smoke your brisket for at least 4 hours, making sure to spray your brisket every hour with some apple juice to keep the brisket tender.

5. After this time wrap your brisket with a sheet of aluminum foil and continue to smoke for the next 3 ½ to 4 ½ hours. Make sure that your smoke your brisket until it reaches an internal temperature of 185 degrees.

6. Remove your brisket and allow to rest for at least 20 minutes before slicing.

7. Next place a skillet over medium or high heat. Add in a tough of oil and once your oil is hot enough add in your garlic. Cook for at least one minute. Remove and allow to cool slight before adding in your butter. Season with a touch of salt and black pepper.

8. Add in your bread slices and grill for at least a minute on each side or until golden brown in color on both sides. Rub your bread slices with your garlic butter.

9. Then make your pickled red onions. To do this use a small sized saucepan and place over medium heat. Add in your vinegar, white sugar, mustard seeds and dash of salt. Stir to combine and bring this mixture to a boil. Cook until your sugar and dash of salt until it fully dissolves.

10. Transfer this mixture to a medium sized bowl and allow to sit for the next 10 minutes. Add in your onions and toss to combine. Cover with a sheet of plastic wrap and place into your fridge to chill for at least an hour.

11. Remove your onions after this time and serve with your freshly smoked brisket and grilled Texas style toast. Enjoy!

Smoked Beef Brisket Tostadas

These tostadas are packed full with some fresh and smooth avocado, fresh lime juice, some fresh cheese, a touch of jalapeno slices and tomatoes. It makes for a delicious smoked lunch meal that you can enjoy any day of the week.

Makes: 4 to 6 Servings

Total Prep Time: 20 Minutes

Ingredients:

- ½ Cup of Salsa, Your Favorite Kind
- 1 Tbsp. of Cilantro, Fresh and Roughly Chopped

- 1, 16 Ounce Can of Bean, Refried Variety and Fat Free
- 6 Tostada Shells, Corn Variety
- 1 Pound of Beef Brisket, Premade and Warm
- ¼ Cup of Red Onion, Finely Chopped

Directions:

1. The first thing that you will want to do is preheat your oven to 400 degrees.

2. While your oven is heating up place your favorite kind of salsa and chopped cilantro. Stir thoroughly to combine.

3. Spread your refried beans on top of your tostada shells.

4. Transfer your shells into a large sized jelly roll pan. Top off with your premade brisket, onion and salsa mixture.

5. Place into your oven to bake for the next 8 to 10 minutes.

6. Remove and serve right away.

Smoked Fireball Whiskey Meatballs

These are delicious and memorable meatballs that I know you are going to want to prepare for every dinner or lunch event that you are hosting. Made with beef and smoked to perfection, this is one meatball dish that you are going to want to enjoy as often as possible.

Makes: 20 Servings

Total Prep Time: 1 Hour and 20 Minutes

Ingredients:

- 1 Cup of Woodchips, Apple Variety
- 1 Cup of Woodchips, Jack Daniels Variety and Smoked

- ½ Cup of Breadcrumbs, Panko Variety
- 1/3 Cup of Milk, Whole
- 2 Tbsp. of Whiskey, Fireball Variety
- ½ Cup of Romano and Pecorino Cheese, Freshly Grated
- ¼ Cup of Parsley, Fresh and Roughly Chopped
- 4 Cloves of Garlic, Minced
- 1 Pound of Beef, Lean and Ground
- 1 Pound of Pork, Lean and Ground
- 12 Ounces of Bacon, Applewood Smoked Variety and Finely Chopped
- 2 tsp. of Salt, For Taste
- 1 tsp. of Black Pepper, For Taste
- 1 tsp. of Red Pepper Flakes, Crushed
- ½ Cup of Barbecue Sauce, Fireball Whiskey Variety

Directions:

1. The first thing that you will want to do is soak your apple and Jack Daniels style wood chips in some water for at least 30 minutes.

2. Then use a large sized bowl and add in your breadcrumbs, whiskey and milk. Stir to combine and allow to sit for at least 5 minutes.

3. After this time add in your grated cheese, fresh parsley, minced garlic, lean beef, lean pork and smoked bacon. Season with a dash of salt and black pepper. Stir to combine. Roll this mixture into even sized balls.

4. Using a smoked preheat your smoker to 300 degrees. Add in your smoked woodchips.

5. Once your smoker has preheat add your meatballs and smoke for at least 30 minutes.

6. After this time brush your meatballs with your barbecue sauce. Cover and continue to smoke for another 15 minutes before brushing with some more sauce. Continue to smoke for another 15 minutes.

7. Remove and serve with some extra barbecue sauce. Enjoy whenever you are ready.

Delicious Smoked Shrimp

If you are a huge fan of shrimp, then this is the perfect recipe for you to make. Smoked to perfection and served with your favorite dipping sauce, this is one dish that will leave your mouth watering.

Makes: 10 Servings

Total Prep Time: 1 Hour and 10 Minutes

Ingredients:

- 3 Pounds of Shrimp, Headless Variety
- 1 ½ Sticks of Butter, Soft
- 1/3 Cup of Worcestershire Sauce
- ¼ Cup of Hot Sauce, Your Favorite Kind and Mild or Medium Heat
- 1 tsp. of Liquid Crab, Boil Variety
- 1/8 Cup of Black Pepper, For Taste
- 1/8 Cup of Cayenne Pepper
- 1 Tbsp. of Basil, Sweet Variety and Fresh
- 1 Tbsp. of Oregano, Fresh and Dried
- 1 tsp. of Cumin, Ground Variety
- 1 tsp. of Paprika
- 1 tsp. of Nutmeg, Ground Variety
- Some Woodchips, Apple Variety

Directions:

1. Place your butter into a large sized baking dish and preheat in your smoker until the butter is fully melted.

2. Once melted add in your Worcestershire sauce, favorite kind of hot sauce and liquid crab boil. Stir to combine. Add in your shrimp and toss to coat in your butter sauce.

3. Next use a small sized bowl and add in your dash of black pepper, dash of cayenne pepper, fresh oregano, fresh basil, ground cumin, dash of paprika and ground nutmeg. Stir to combine and season your coated shrimp with this mixture.

4. Preheat your smoker to 225 to 230 degrees. While your smoker is preheating and add in your apple style woodchips.

5. Once your smoker is hot enough add in your shrimp. Smoke for the next 45 minutes to an hour or until your shrimp begins to turn opaque. Make sure that you flip your shrimp at least halfway through.

6. Place your shrimp into a large sized bowl and pour some of your leftover sauce over the top. Serve right away and enjoy.

Thanksgiving Smoked Turkey

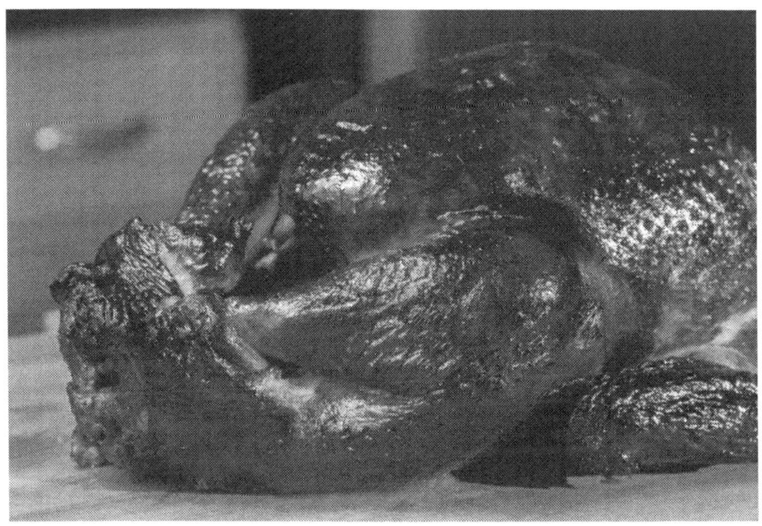

If you ae looking for the ultimate Thanksgiving turkey recipe to make that will certainly impress your friends and family during the holidays, this is one turkey dish that you can't go wrong with. Smoked and absolutely delicious, this is one turkey dish that you may not have leftovers with.

Makes: 8 Servings

Total Prep Time: 6 Hours

Ingredients:

- 2 Cups of Apple Juice, Fresh
- 2 Cups of Water, Warm
- 1, 19 Pound Turkey, Frozen and thawed

- 1 Cup of Seasoning, Cajun Variety
- Some Marinade, Your Favorite Kind and For Injection

Directions:

1. Use a large sized water tray and fill at least halfway with your apple juice and water. Stir to combine.

2. Meanwhile preheat your smoker to 275 degrees.

3. Next pat dry your turkey with some paper towels.

4. Using a marinade injector, inject your favorite marinade into your turkey and then season the outside of it with your Cajun seasoning.

5. Place your turkey inside of your smoker along with your water try filled with apple juice mixture. Smoke for the next 5 ½ hours or until the internal temperature is 165 degrees.

6. After this time remove and allow to sit for the next 10 minutes before carving and serving.

Smoked Shrimp Po' Boys Smothered in Remoulade Sauce

This is an excellent recipe to make that can pair excellently with the smoked shrimp recipe inside of this book. Make this delicious sandwich recipe whenever you need something savory to enjoy.

Makes: 6 Servings

Total Prep Time: 1 Hour and 15 Minutes

Ingredients:

- 4 Tbsp. of Shrimp Boil, Liquid
- 3 Bay Leaves, Fresh and Dried
- ½ Cup of Water, Warm
- 4 Pounds of Shrimp, Large in Size, Peeled, Deveined and Washed
- 3 Lemons, Fresh and Juice Only
- ½ Cup of Butter, Soft
- 1 Tbsp. of Worcestershire Sauce
- 1 Tbsp. of Cajun Seasoning
- 1 Tbsp. of Pepper, Garlic Variety
- 6 Buns, Po' Boy Variety or French
- 3 Tomatoes, Large in Size and Sliced Thinly
- 2 Cups of Pickles, Dill Variety and Sliced Thinly

Ingredients for Your Remoulade Sauce:

- ¼ Cup of Oil, Vegetable Variety
- ¼ Cup of Mayonnaise, Your Favorite Kind
- 2 Tbsp. of Mustard, Creole Variety

- 2 Tbsp. of Horseradish Sauce
- 2 Tbsp. of Lemon Juice, Fresh
- 1 Tbsp. of Parsley, Fresh and Roughly Chopped
- 2 tsp. of Vinegar, Red Wine Variety
- 1 tsp. of Paprika
- 2 ½ tsp. of Garlic, Freshly Minced

Directions:

1. Using a large sized water tray add in your liquid shrimp, warm water and dried bay leaves. Then preheat your smoked to 250 degrees.

2. Meanwhile place your shrimp into a large sized baking dish. Drizzle your fresh lemon juice over the top. Set aside for later use.

3. Use a small sized saucepan and place over medium heat. Add in your butter and once it is fully melted add in your Worcestershire sauce, dried Cajun seasoning and garlic style pepper. Mix well to combine. Pour this mixture over your shrimp and toss to combine.

4. Place your shrimp into a preheated smoker. Smoke at 225 degrees for the next 50 minutes. After this time remove your shrimp from your smoked and place into your oven to broil for at least 3 minutes. Remove from heat and set aside for later use.

5. Next make your remoulade sauce. To do this use a food processor and add in your oil, favorite kind of mayonnaise, mustard, horseradish, fresh lemon juice, fresh parsley, vinegar, paprika and minced garlic. Blend on the highest setting until smooth in consistency.

6. Spread your freshly made remoulade sauce on both sides of your buns. Place a piece of shredded lettuce on each slice of bread along with slices of dill pickles and tomatoes. Top off with your smoked shrimp. Place your sandwich together and enjoy right away.

Delicious Smoked Stuffed Salmon

This is the ultimate smoked recipe to make if you are a huge fan of salmon. Make this dish whenever you are looking for a filling meal to make for your significant other on a special occasion.

Makes: 2 Servings

Total Prep Time: 3 to 4 Hours

Ingredients:

- 4 to 5 Pounds of Salmon, Fresh and Wild Caught Variety
- 3 Tbsp. of Oil, Extra Virgin Variety
- ¼ Cup of Green Onions, Fresh and Roughly Chopped
- 1 Cup of Tomato, Peeled and Finely Chopped
- ¼ Cup of Dill, Roughly Chopped and Fresh
- ½ Cup of Bread Cubes, Dried
- ¼ Cup of Celery, Fresh and Thinly Sliced
- ¼ tsp. of Salt, For Taste
- ½ tsp. of Pepper, Lemon Variety and For Taste
- 1 Clove of Garlic, Minced

Directions:

1. The first thing that you will want to do is brush your salmon with a generous amount of olive oil.

2. Then add in your remaining ingredients into a small sized bowl. Stir thoroughly to combine.

3. Slice your salmon right in the middle to form a pocket. Stuff your salmon with your herb mixture until your mixture has been fully used. Transfer to a large sized baking sheet lined with a sheet of aluminum foil.

4. Place into a preheated smoker with some apple woodchips. Smoke at 225 degrees for the next 3 to 4 hours or until fully cooked through.

5. Remove and serve whenever you are ready. Enjoy.

Smoked Lamb Legs

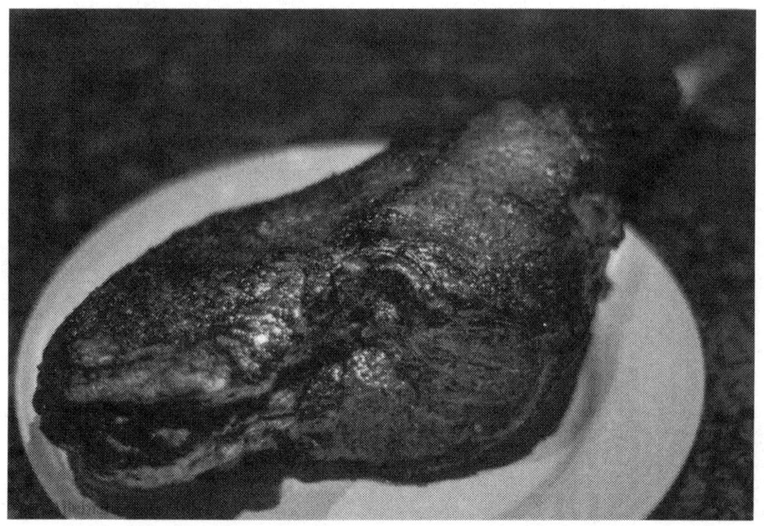

This is a smoked recipe you are going to love if you are looking for something more on the exotic side to enjoy. This smoked lamb leg recipe is great when paired with some Texas toast or a side of mashed potatoes.

Makes: 1 Serving

Total Prep Time: 2 to 3 ½ Hours

Ingredients:

- 4 Cups of Woodchips, Apple or Cherry Variety
- 1, 5 to 6 Pound Leg of Lamb, Whole
- ½ Cup of Whipping Cream, Heavy Variety

- 1 Tbsp. of Mustard, Dijon Variety
- 1 tsp. of Rosemary, Fresh and Roughly Chopped
- Dash of Black Pepper, For Taste and Optional

Directions:

1. At least an hour before you smoke your lamb leg, you will want to make sure to soak your woodchips in some water. After this time drain your woodchips and sprinkle half onto your smoke. Cover and preheat your smoke to at least 220 to 300 degrees.

2. While your smoker is heating up and your leg of lamb and cover. Allow to smoke for the next 1 to 2 ½ hours or until done to your desire. Make sure that you add more woodchips halfway through the cooking process.

3. Meanwhile use a small sized bowl and add in your heavy whipping cream. Use an electric mixer and beat until thick in consistency. Add in your Dijon style mustard and fresh rosemary. Beat again until incorporated.

4. Serve your leg of lamb and serve with a dollop of your cream over the top. Season with some pepper and serve whenever you are ready.

Smoked Weekend Gumbo

If you are looking for a delicious and filling dish to make during the weekend that will leave you feeling warm, then this is the perfect dish for you to make. It is relatively easy to make and will leave you feeling full and satisfied.

Makes: 4 Servings

Total Prep Time: 4 Hours

Ingredients:

- 1, 4 Pound Chicken, Whole and Split
- 2 Tbsp. of Olive Oil, Extra Virgin Variety

- ½ tsp. of Meat Tenderizer, Your Favorite Kind and Evenly Divided
- 2, 5 Ounce Packs of Gumbo Mix, Louisiana Variety
- 1 Cup of Celery, Fresh and Thinly Sliced
- 1 ¾ Cups of Okra, Thinly Sliced
- 2 tsp. of Garlic, Minced
- ½ Cup of Green Onions, Fresh Thinly Sliced
- ½ Cup of Onion, Sweet Variety and Finely Chopped
- 1 tsp. of Liquid Shrimp Boil
- 1 Pound of Sausage, Turkey Variety
- Some French Bread, For Serving

Directions:

1. The first thing that you will want to do is preheat a smoker to 250 degrees.

2. While your smoker is heating up pierce each half of your chicken with a fork all over the surface. Then baste each side with a generous amount of olive oil before seasoning with your meat tenderizer.

3. Place your chicken into your smoker and smoke for the next 2 to 3 ½ hours or until your chicken is fully cooked through.

4. While your chicken is smoking use a large sized stockpot and prepare your gumbo mix according to the directions on the package. Once your gumbo is fully cooked through add in your fresh celery, okra, minced garlic, fresh green onions, sweet style onion and liquid shrimp boil. Stir to thoroughly combine.

5. Bring your gumbo to a boil before reducing the heat to medium or low. Allow to simmer for the next 15 minutes.

6. Once your chicken is fully cooked through remove it from your smoker and allow to cool. Once cooled pull the meat from the bone.

7. Slice your turkey sausage into thin sized slices. Add both your pulled chicken and sausage slices into your gumbo. Stir to incorporate and cook over low heat for the next 20 minutes.

8. After this time add in your rice and cook for another 15 minutes. After this time fluff with a fork. Remove from heat and allow to sit for at least 5 minutes before serving it with your French bread. Enjoy while still piping hot.

Delicious Smoked Chicken Wings

This is the perfect dish to serve up during the football season. For the tastiest results don't hesitate to serve this chicken wings with your favorite dipping sauces.

Makes: 4 Servings

Total Prep Time: 2 Hours

Ingredients:

- 4 Pounds of Chicken Wings
- 1 Bottle of Italian Dressing, Your Favorite Kind
- Some Dry Rub, Your Favorite Kind

Directions:

1. Twenty-four hours before making it clean and separate your chicken wings under some water. Pat dry with a paper towels and place into a large sized Ziploc bag. Add in your Dressing and toss to coat.

2. The next day rinse your chicken wings under some running and water pat dry with a paper towel.

3. Place back into a large sized Ziploc bag and add in your favorite kind of dry rub. Toss thoroughly to coat.

4. Then preheat a smoker to 300 to 325 degrees. Once your smoker is hot enough add in your chicken wings and smoke for the next 1 to 1 ½ hours.

5. Remove after this time and serve right away.

Smoked Egg Salad Sandwiches

If you are looking for a simple sandwich recipe to make whenever you are tight on time, then this is the perfect sandwich recipe for you. Smoky in taste and ready in just a couple of minutes, this is the perfect dish to make during the week.

Makes: 4 Servings

Total Prep Time: 2 Hours and 20 Minutes

Ingredients:

- 8 Eggs, Large in Size and Smoked Variety
- ½ Cup of Mayonnaise, Your Favorite Kind
- 1 tsp. of Mustard, Spicy Variety
- ¼ Cup of Scallions, Finely Chopped
- ¼ Cup of Paprika, Smoked Variety
- Dash of Salt and Black Pepper, For Taste
- 4 Rolls, Hawaiian Style

Directions:

1. The first thing that you will want to do is smoke your eggs. To do this use a preheated smoker set to 225 degrees and add in your eggs. Smoke for at least 2 hours. After this time peel the shells and chop your eggs finely.

2. Add your chopped eggs along with your remaining ingredients into a medium sized bowl. Stir thoroughly to combine.

3. Spread your mixture on your Hawaiian style rolls and top off with the tops. Serve right away and enjoy.

Alabama Style Pulled Pork

This pulled pork recipe is perfect to make during your next family cookout. For the tastiest results make sure that you use either pork shoulder or pork butt. Regardless this make the most delicious pulled pork you will ever taste.

Makes: 16 Servings

Total Prep Time: 1 Day and 12 Hours

Ingredients:

- 3 Cups of Vinegar, Apple Cider Variety
- ¼ Cup of Salt, For Taste
- ¼ Cup of Brown Sugar, Light and Packed
- 4 Tbsp. of Black Pepper, For Taste
- 2 Tbsp. of Cayenne Pepper
- ¼ Pound of Butter, Soft
- 1 Quart of Water, Warm
- 5 Pounds of Pork Butt Roast, Boston Variety

Directions:

1. Using a medium sized saucepan add in your vinegar, dash of salt, light brown sugar, dash of black pepper, cayenne pepper and soft butter. Stir this mixture to combine and bring to a boil over medium to high heat.

2. Once your mixture is boiling add in your water and bring back to a boil. Remove from heat and set aside for later use.

3. Place your pork butt onto a preheated smoker set to 230 to 300 degrees. Add in some soaked hickory woodchips and smoke for the next 6 to 10 hours or until your pork is fully cooked through. As your pork is smoking, baste it with your premade sauce every 30 minutes to an hour.

4. Remove your pork from the smoker and wrap in a sheet of aluminum foil. Prior to sealing the aluminum foil, pour your remaining sauce over the top and seal.

5. Place your pork back onto your smoker and heat to 350 degrees. Continue to smoke for the next 2 hours. Once done remove and allow to stand for at least 10 minutes. After this time remove the meat from the bone and shred finely using two forks.

6. Serve your pork immediately and enjoy.

Sweet Smoked Pork Ribs

While pork ribs are delicious on their own, these ribs are one of the best rib recipes that you will get the chance to taste. Sweet in flavor and packed with a smoky taste, this is a filling rib dish that will also satisfy your strongest sweet tooth.

Makes: 10 Servings

Total Prep Time: 5 Hours

Ingredients:

- ¼ Cup of Salt, For Taste
- ¼ Cup of Sugar, White in Color
- 2 Tbsp. of Brown Sugar, Light and Packed
- 2 Tbsp. of Black Pepper, For Taste
- 2 Tbsp. of Pepper, White in Color and For Taste
- 2 Tbsp. of Onion, Powdered Variety
- 1 Tbsp. of Garlic, Powdered Variety
- 1 Tbsp. of Chili, Powdered Variety
- 1 Tbsp. of Paprika
- 1 Tbsp. of Cumin, Ground Variety
- 10 Pounds of Pork Ribs, Baby Back Variety
- 1 Cup of Apple Juice, Fresh
- ¼ Cup of Brown Sugar, Light and Packed
- ¼ Cup of Barbecue Sauce, Your Favorite Kind

Directions:

1. First use a small sized bowl and add in your dash of salt, white sugar, light brown sugar, dash of black pepper, dash of white pepper, powdered onion, powdered garlic, powdered chili, paprika and ground cumin. Stir thoroughly to combine.

2. Rub your freshly made spice mixture over the entire surface of your ribs. Wrap your ribs in a sheet of plastic and place into your fridge to sit for the next 30 minutes.

3. After this time place your ribs into a preheat smoker set to 270 degrees. Make sure that you fill your smoker with presoaked apple woodchips. Smoke your ribs for at least an hour.

4. While your ribs are smoking add your fresh apple juice, light brown sugar and favorite kind of barbecue sauce into a medium sized bowl. Stir thoroughly to combine and brush your ribs with this sauce during the first 30 minutes during the first hour.

5. Continue to smoke your ribs for the next 3 to 4 hours, making sure to baste it with your sauce every 30 minutes.

6. Once your ribs are fully cooked wrap them in a sheet of aluminum foil. Allow to rest for the next 10 to 15 minutes before serving.

Classic Smoked Salmon

This is the perfect smoked recipe to make if you are a huge fan of salmon. One bite from this fish and I know you will want to make it over and over again.

Makes: 10 Servings

Total Prep Time: 4 Hours and 55 Minutcs

Ingredients:

- ½ Cup of Brown Sugar, Light and Packed
- 2 Tbsp. of Salt, For Taste
- 2 Tbsp. of Red Pepper Flakes, Crushed Variety
- ½ Cup of Mint Leaves, Fresh and Roughly Chopped

- ¼ Cup of Brandy, Your Favorite Kind
- 1, 4 Pound of Salmon, Bones Removed
- 2 Cups of Woodchips, Alder Variety and Presoaked

Directions:

1. Use a small sized bowl and add in your light brown sugar, dash of salt, crushed red pepper, fresh mint leaves and brandy. Stir thoroughly until a paste begins to form.

2. Rub this freshly made paste all over the surface of your salmon. Wrap your salmon in a sheet of plastic wrap and place into your fridge to marinate for the next 4 hours.

3. Preheat an outdoor grill to high heat. Place your soaked woodchips into a deposable over pan and place under the grate of your grill.

4. Add in your salmon and close the lid. Cook for the next 45 minutes or until your salmon turns red brown in color.

5. Remove and allow to sit for the next 5 minutes before serving.

Texas Style Smoked Flounder

There is nothing that taste better during the summer holidays more so then this smoked flounder recipe. It is a great dish to make if you are a novice to smoking as it is relatively easy to prepare.

Makes: 2 Servings

Total Prep Time: 40 Minutes

Ingredients:

- 1 Flounder, Whole
- 1 Lemon, Fresh and Cut In Half

- Dash of Black pepper, For Taste
- 2 Tbsp. of Dill, Fresh and Roughly Chopped
- 1 Tbsp. of Olive Oil, Extra Virgin Variety
- 1 Cup of Woodchips, Hickory Variety and Soaked

Directions:

1. The first thing that you will want to do is preheat a smoker to 350 degrees. Add in your presoaked woodchips and cover your smoker.

2. While your smoker is preheating clean and scale your flounder. Then slice your lemon into thin slices and rub a generous amount of olive oil over your fish. Season with a dash of black and pepper and stuff your flounder with your fresh dill. Stuff with some fresh lemon slices.

3. Place your flounder onto a large sheet of aluminum foil and fold the sides around your fish.

4. Place your flounder into your smoker and close the lid. Smoke your flounder for about 10 minutes before folding your foil into a packet. Continue to smoke for the next 20 minutes or until your flounder is fully cooked through.

5. Remove after this time and garnish with some additional dill. Serve right away and enjoy.

Maple Style Smoked Prime Rib

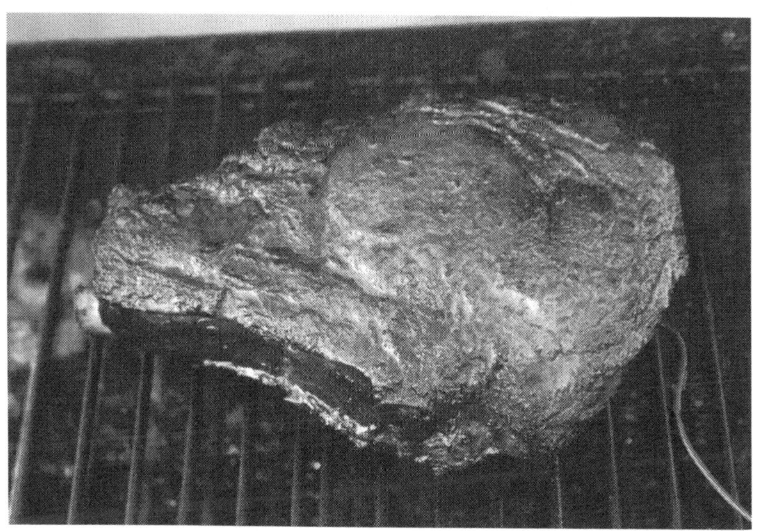

If you are looking for a savory smoked recipe to make that will impress your friends and family, then this is the perfect dish for you to make. It is easy to prepare and will leave your family craving for more.

Makes: 8 Servings

Total Prep Time: 1 Hour and 18 Minutes

Ingredients:

- 3 Cups of Woodchips, Maple Variety
- 1, 6 Pound Standing Rib, Bones Separate and Tied in Place

- Dash of Sea Salt, Coarse Variety and For Taste
- Dash of Black Pepper, For Taste

Directions:

1. The first thing that you will want to do is soak your woodchips in water for at least an hour until thoroughly soaked.

2. Then preheat a smoker to 225 degrees. While your smoker is heating up place a drip pan underneath the rack of your smoker.

3. Season your roast with a generous amount of sea salt and black pepper, making sure to season all sides of your roast. Place into your preheated smoker and cover.

4. Roast for at least 30 minutes before adding more woodchips. Continue to smoke for another 30 minutes and add in your remaining chips. Continue to smoke until thoroughly brown on all sides. This should take at least 2 more hours.

5. Remove after this time and transfer to a cutting board. Cover with a sheet of aluminum foil and allow to rest for 30 minutes before carving into thin slices. Serve whenever you are ready and enjoy.

Sweet Smoked Honey Turkey

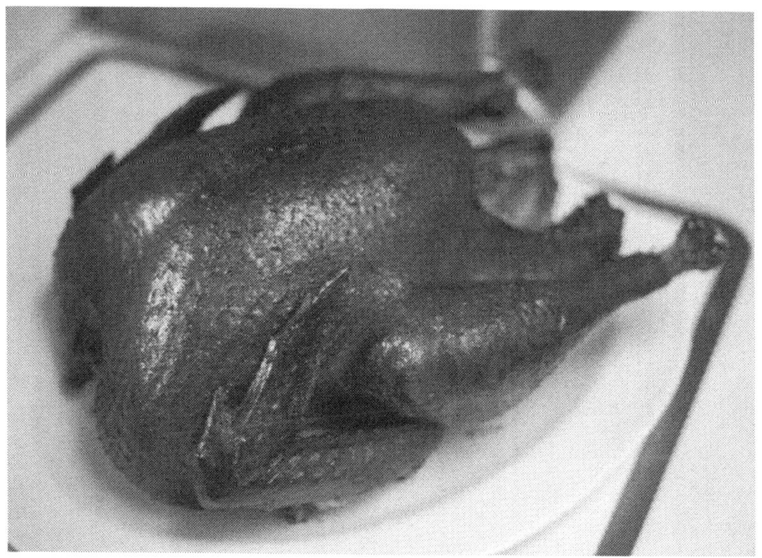

With the help of this delicious smoked turkey recipe, Thanksgiving will never be the same again. This recipe makes such a delicious turkey, you will never want to make another turkey during the holidays again.

Makes: 16 Servings

Total Prep Time: 3 Hours and 45 Minutes

Ingredients:

- 1, 12 Pound Turkey, Whole
- 2 Tbsp. of Sage, Fresh and Roughly Chopped
- 2 Tbsp. of Black Pepper, For Taste

- 2 Tbsp. of Salt, Celery Variety
- 2 Tbsp. of Basil, Fresh and Roughly Chopped
- 2 Tbsp. of Oil, Vegetable Variety
- 1, 12 Ounce Jar of Honey, Raw
- ½ Pound of Woodchips, Mesquite Variety

Directions:

1. The first thing that you will want to do is preheat a grill to high heat. While your grill is heating up soak your woodchips in a large sized pan of water. Set aside for later use.

2. Then remove your neck and giblets from your turkey. Rinse under some running water and pat dry with a few paper towels. Place into a large sized roasting pan.

3. Use a medium sized bowl and add in your fresh sage, dash of black pepper, dash of celery style salt, fresh basil and vegetable oil. Stir thoroughly to combine and pour this mixture over your turkey. Turn your turkey over and tent a sheet of aluminum foil over your turkey.

4. Place your turkey onto your preheated grill. Add a handful of your soaked wood chips onto your hot coal. Cover and smoke for the next hour.

5. After this time add more of your soaked woodchip onto your coals.

6. Drizzle half of your honey over your turkey and cover with your aluminum foil again. Cover and continue to smoke for the next 1 ½ to 2 hours or until your chicken is fully cooked through.

7. Uncover your turkey and baste with your remaining honey. Continue to cook for another 15 minutes.

8. Remove and allow to stand for at least 10 minutes before serving.

Conclusion

Well, there you have it!

Hopefully by the end of this book you have become a professional meat smoker! I hope that by the end of this book I hope that not only have you learned how to smoke your own meat in a simple step-by-step fashion, but have also learned a few helpful tips along the way. I also hope that with the help of the over 25 delicious smoked meat recipes you have found in this book, you have learned how to accomplish just that.

So, what is next for you?

The next step for you to take is to actually get out there and begin smoking your own meat. Remember to use your favorite kind of marinades when prepping your meat and to take the initiative to making your own smoked meat recipes from scratch.

Don't worry. I have complete faith in you.

Good luck!

About the Author

Hello my name is Ted Alling,

For as long as I can remember, I have always loved cooking and spending time in the kitchen. I honestly thought that my mother had dedicated her life to cooking, but later on in life, I came to understand that she was just a great stay at home mom of 4. Although I was a boy, I was always the only one interested in helping my mom make pancakes, fried eggs, and bratwurst. She proceeded to teach me how to make pasta, to cook chicken, stuff cabbages, and even how to make a pretty good risotto.

Life in Germany was wonderful as a kid, but my parents decided to move to the United States, or more specifically to the state of Illinois, in 1990. When I moved out to go to college in Georgia, not only was I able to make some delicious dishes, but I was a very popular roommate to have—I was one of the very rare ones who could prepare something other than mac & cheese from the box. The other students from the dorm really dug my special fried rice. Until this day, I won't give out the secret ingredient that makes it unique…

I graduated from college with honors and an accounting degree in 1995, and soon after started working in a firm in downtown Atlanta. All I could think about all day was what I would make for my girlfriend for dinner. She obviously did not mind that I had taken over the kitchen early on in our relationship. She is a nurse, and often has to work long hours and comes home exhausted and hungry.

However, food had become much more than a hobby or necessity for me…it was actually closer to an obsession, but I prefer to use the term passion. I was spending most of my weekends visiting fresh local markets and discovering new produce and herbs. After working as an accountant for 5 years, I realized that life was far too short to continue missing out on my true calling: cooking.

I applied as a part time cook at a local diner about 10 minutes from home, and the rest, as they say, is history. Three years later I was opening my own restaurant with my wife as my main partner. All my ex-fellow accountants now come in to eat at lunch time. We have been serving our clientele my famous fried rice, and many more dishes that I will be glad to share with you over the future weeks.

What makes me a good chef? My passion for food, and the fresher the ingredients, the better. I love to experiment with flavors and I dare you to do the same. Sure, we all have our favorites, but don't settle in your ways. Be creative. Play with the colors, the herbs, the spices, the types of meat, fruits, and vegetables. Grow your own garden and talk to your butcher about trying different cuts of meat that he has to offer on a weekly basis.

Now, I have to go back to the kitchen, but next time you feel like preparing a mouthwatering dish, please stop by, and I will make sure to share "most" of my secrets.

Author's Afterthoughts

Thanks ever so much to each of my cherished readers for investing the time to read this book!

I know you could have picked from many other books but you chose this one. So a big thanks for downloading this book and reading all the way to the end.

If you enjoyed this book or received value from it, I'd like to ask you for a favor. Please take a few minutes to post an honest and heartfelt review on Amazon.com. Your support does make a difference and helps to benefit other people.

Thanks!

Ted Alling

Made in the USA
Lexington, KY
23 January 2017